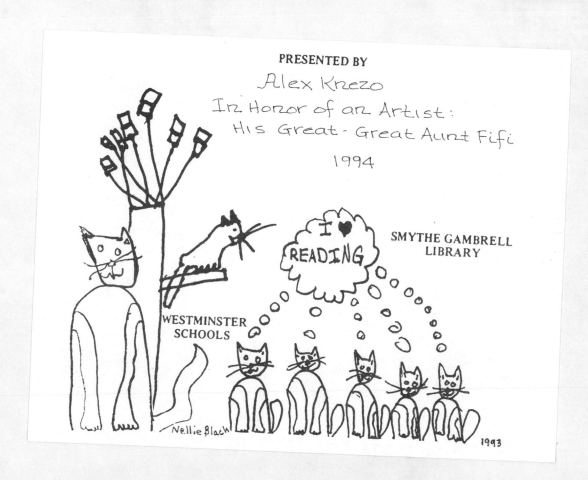

Color

Hilary Devonshire

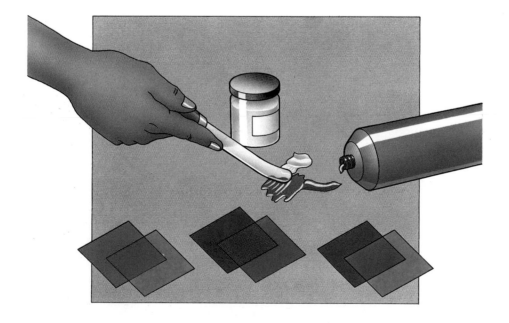

FRANKLIN WATTS

New York/London/Toronto/Sydney

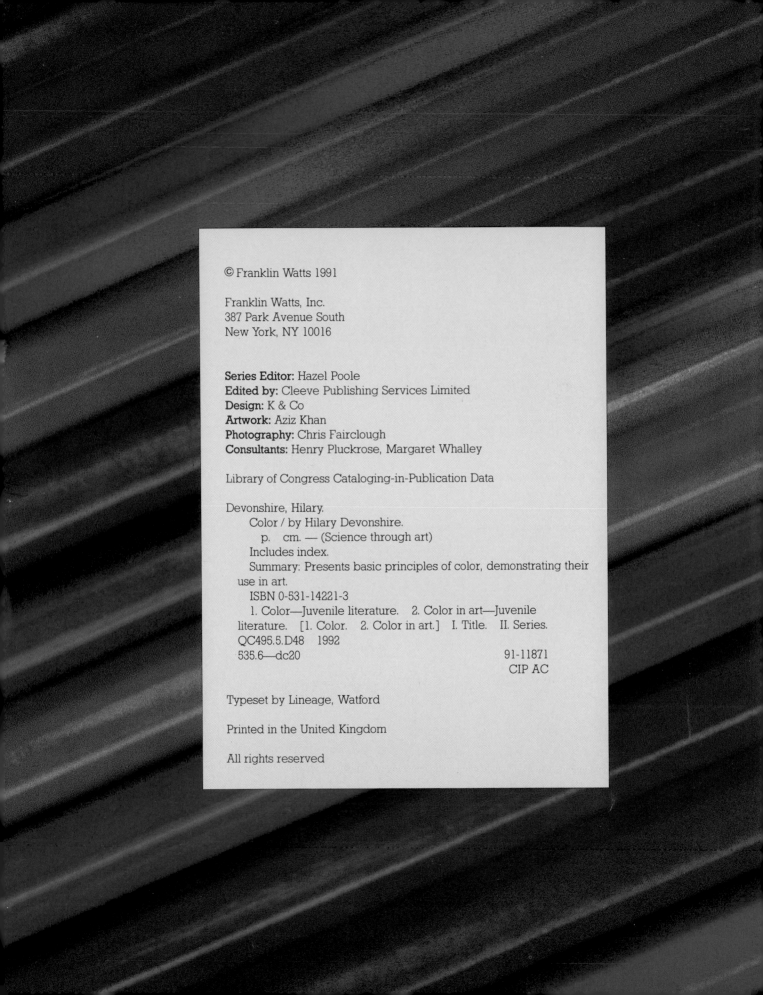

© Franklin Watts 1991

Franklin Watts, Inc.
387 Park Avenue South
New York, NY 10016

Series Editor: Hazel Poole
Edited by: Cleeve Publishing Services Limited
Design: K & Co
Artwork: Aziz Khan
Photography: Chris Fairclough
Consultants: Henry Pluckrose, Margaret Whalley

Library of Congress Cataloging-in-Publication Data

Devonshire, Hilary.
     Color / by Hilary Devonshire.
          p.   cm. — (Science through art)
     Includes index.
     Summary: Presents basic principles of color, demonstrating their
use in art.
     ISBN 0-531-14221-3
     1. Color—Juvenile literature.   2. Color in art—Juvenile
literature.   [1. Color.   2. Color in art.]   I. Title.   II. Series.
QC495.5.D48   1992
535.6—dc20   91-11871
                                                              CIP AC

Typeset by Lineage, Watford

Printed in the United Kingdom

CONTENTS

EQUIPMENT AND MATERIALS

This book describes activities which use the following:

Adhesive tape, double-sided
Adhesives (white, cold-water paste)
Apron
Black colors (inks, paints, pens)
Bowl
Camera
Cardboard (white)
Cellophane sheets (or acetate or plastic)
Compass
Cooking fat
Dishwashing liquid
Drinking straws
Fabrics – plain, cotton
        – printed, colored
Felt-tip pens
Iron
Leaves
Light scope
Magazine (for pictures)
Magnifying glass
Paintbrush
Paints – acryclic paints
        – oil paints
        – powder paints
        – watercolor paints

Palette (or plate)
Paper – black paper
       – blotting paper
       – colored paper
       – construction paper (various colors)
       – tissue paper (various colors)
       – white paper
Pebbles (or marbles)
Pencil
Plant materials (roots, leaves, fruit, or bark)
Plant support sticks
Prism (triangular, glass)
Rubber bands
Rubber gloves
Ruler
Saucepan (old)
Scissors
String (thin)
Sunglasses
Water
Wax crayons
Wood (an old branch, small twigs)
Wood ash

All the colors of the rainbow are contained in the white light of the sun, and because our eyes are sensitive to different colors in light we can see these colors all around us. We can see many different colors, but not every animal can see color. Horses, dogs, cats and cows see the world in black, gray and white. Reptiles, birds, insects and fish can see in color, like human beings.

When we look at different objects, we see them in different colors. This is because when light shines on an object only some of the color in light is reflected back into our eyes and the other colors are absorbed by the object. A red car reflects back the red color in light, so it looks red. White things reflect all the colors in light; black things absorb all the colors – they reflect no light.

Color has many uses. You will learn about these as you work through this book. In nature, animals and plants use color. Sometimes they use it to camouflage themselves — they hide from enemies. Sometimes they use bright colors to attract attention. We use colors too. Red is often used as a warning color. It is used for traffic lights and signs to tell us to stop. It is used in flags on beaches to tell us not to swim.

Did you know that light travels in

waves? Think of the ripples that form when you drop a pebble in still water. The waves spread out in rings from their source and are different lengths, or wavelengths. Our eyes are sensitive to the different wavelengths in light, and so we can see different colors. But we can only detect the light rays in the middle of the band of wavelengths. We call this the visible spectrum. Ultraviolet rays have shorter wavelengths, and we cannot see them. They are used in medicine and X-rays. Infrared rays have longer wavelengths, and are used in night photography and electronics. The remote control units of television sets and VCRs work using infrared light.

By following the investigations in this book you will learn something about the science of color. At the start of each section there are some scientific ideas

to be explored. A scientist looks at ideas and tries to discover if they are always true, and will also investigate to see if they can be *disproved.* You will be working like a scientist. A scientist is curious and wants to find out about the world in which we live. A scientist tests ideas, makes investigations and experiments, and tries to explain what has happened. Your results may be surprising or unexpected, and you may find that you will need to carry out a new investigation, or test a new idea.

You will also be an artist. You will be using color in the art activities that are included in each section. Through working with both color and the various art materials and techniques, you will make discoveries about the nature of color and how color can be used. Your finished pieces of art will be a record of your scientific findings.

COLORS IN LIGHT

White light contains all the colors in the visible spectrum – red, orange, yellow, green, blue, indigo, and violet. Each color has a different wavelength. If a beam of light passes through a glass surface at an angle, it bends (it is refracted). If it passes through the sides of a triangular prism, it is bent twice and the different light wavelengths are separated. You can see the colors of the rainbow.

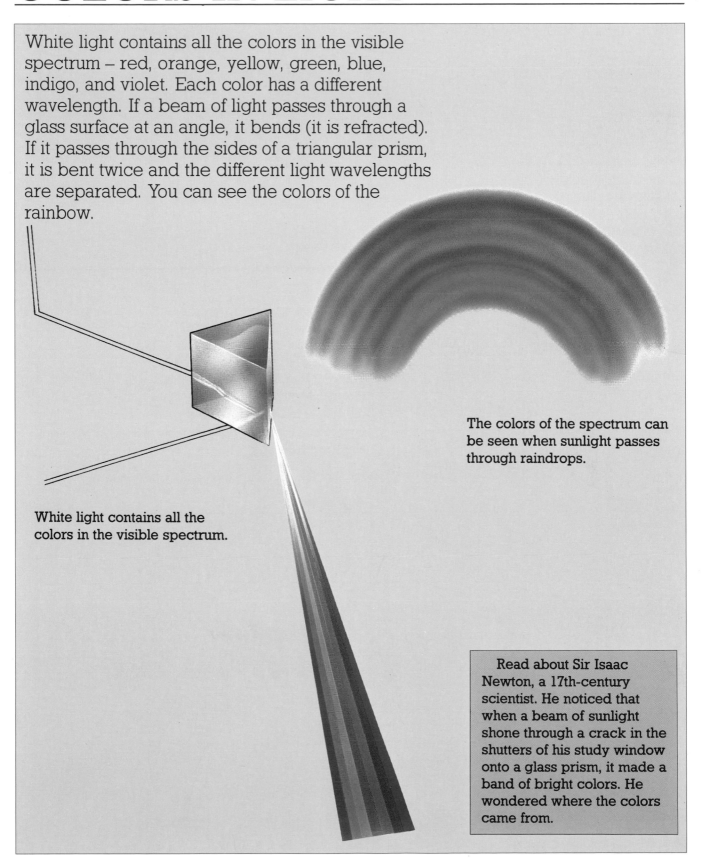

The colors of the spectrum can be seen when sunlight passes through raindrops.

White light contains all the colors in the visible spectrum.

Read about Sir Isaac Newton, a 17th-century scientist. He noticed that when a beam of sunlight shone through a crack in the shutters of his study window onto a glass prism, it made a band of bright colors. He wondered where the colors came from.

Rainbow art

You will need: white paper, wax crayons, black India ink, a paintbrush, an iron, some newspapers.

1. Draw and color a rainbow picture using wax crayons in the colors of the spectrum. Remember to use your crayons in the right order – red, orange, yellow, green, blue, indigo, violet.

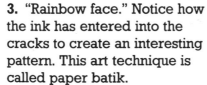

2. Crumple your picture into a ball, then smooth it out again. Spread the newspaper on the table for protection. Brush India ink firmly into the cracks of the crayon picture. The creases can then be removed by ironing your picture between two sheets of clean paper.

3. "Rainbow face." Notice how the ink has entered into the cracks to create an interesting pattern. This art technique is called paper batik.

The human eye is able to detect differences in the wavelengths of light. Different cells in the retina at the back of the eye are sensitive to the red, green and blue colors in light. The retina can also detect black and white so that when you go out at night and there is little light, you can still see things but they appear to be black, white and gray.

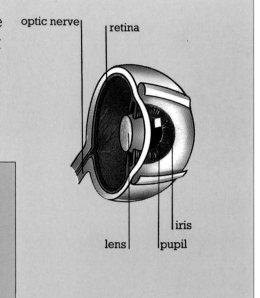

This drawing shows the parts of the eye.

Go outside after dark. What colors can you see? Look again in the daylight and notice how the colors have changed. Ask a doctor or a nurse what tests they might use to discover whether a person is color blind. A color blind person cannot distinguish between certain colors, for example red and green.

Read about Georges Seurat, the famous French artist. He developed a technique called "pointilism" — painting with small dots. He also studied the science of color and optics, the science of vision.

Painting with dots

You will need: white paper, drinking straws (or a plant support stick), red, green and blue paints.

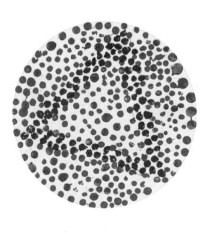

1. Draw a circle on a piece of paper. Use a small piece of straw (or stick) to mark the circumference with green dots of paint. Draw a triangle inside the circle and outline this with dots, too.

2. Fill in the triangle with red dots and the background with green dots. Some people find it difficult to distinguish between red and green. Ask your friends if they can see the triangle.

3. "Fish." Draw a picture using dots. Use only the red, green and blue paints. Notice here how the impression of purple is given where the red and blue dots are close together.

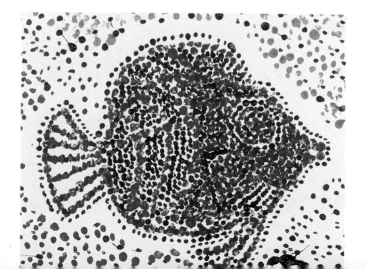

Background color affects the colors you see

You will need: construction paper in a range of colors, and scissors.

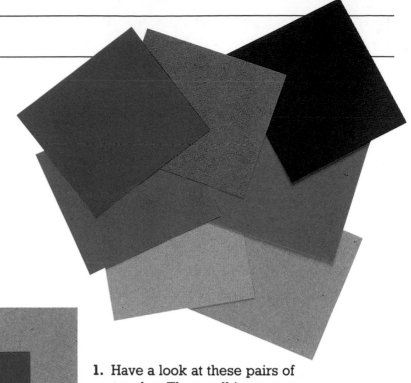

1. Have a look at these pairs of rectangles. The small inner rectangle appears to be a different color from the one next to it because it has been placed on a different background. They are really the same color.

 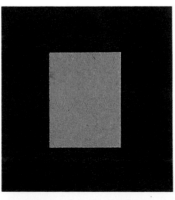

2. Experiment with your paper. Cut two small rectangles of one color and place them on two contrasting background colors. Do they look different?

MIXING LIGHT COLORS

Red, green and blue are the primary light colors. By mixing these colors we can make other colors. Red and green light mixed together make yellow; green and blue light together make cyan (a turquoise color); and red and blue light make magenta (a deep, purplish red). Yellow, cyan and magenta are the secondary colors of light.

When the three primary light colors – red, green and blue – are mixed together in equal proportions they re-form into white light again.

Look at a color television screen through a magnifying glass. The picture is made up of areas of red, green and blue. Your brain mixes the colors so you see many different colors. Use a light scope to look closely at a color magazine picture. What colors do you see?

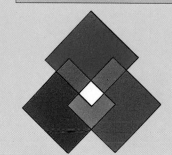

Color spinners

You will need: a compass, white cardboard, a pencil, ruler, thin string, red, blue and green felt-tip pens, scissors.

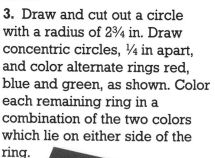

2. Color one circle red, blue and green in equal proportions.

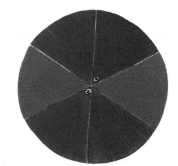

3. Draw and cut out a circle with a radius of 2¾ in. Draw concentric circles, ¼ in apart, and color alternate rings red, blue and green, as shown. Color each remaining ring in a combination of the two colors which lie on either side of the ring.

1. Draw and cut out several circles from the white cardboard. Color the circles in different combinations of colors. Use only two colors at a time.

4. Make two holes on either side of the cardboard circle (approximately ¼ in apart). Thread a piece of string through the holes, and tie it in a loop.

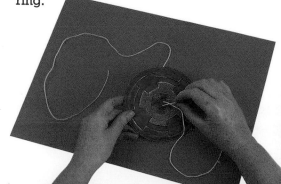

5. Relax and tighten the string to spin your disk.

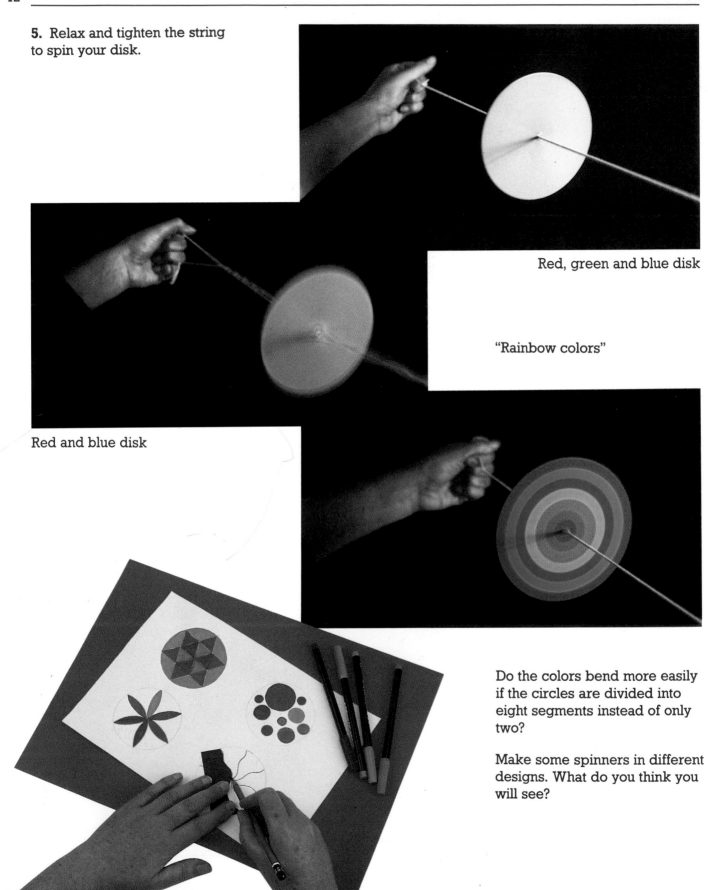

Red, green and blue disk

"Rainbow colors"

Red and blue disk

Do the colors bend more easily if the circles are divided into eight segments instead of only two?

Make some spinners in different designs. What do you think you will see?

FILTERING LIGHT

If you look through a colored filter (a transparent colored sheet of plastic cellophane or glass) the colors that you see will change. This is because the filter will only allow light of its own color to pass through.

A red filter will only let red light through. If you look at a red object through a red filter it becomes pale because the red light has traveled through the filter.

Put on a pair of sunglasses. Notice how the colors that you see change. Sunglasses protect your eyes from bright sunlight. They filter out the glare. When you visit the theater, notice how colored filters are used for stage lighting.

WARNING: NEVER LOOK DIRECTLY AT THE SUN THROUGH A FILTER OR SUNGLASSES. IT IS DANGEROUS AND CAN DAMAGE YOUR EYES.

Looking at a strawberry through a red filter.

Using color filters

You will need: white paper, felt-tip pens, some colored cellophane, plastic or acetate sheets.

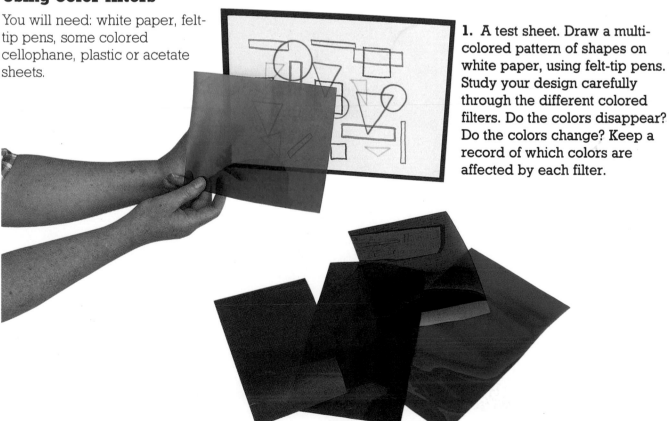

1. A test sheet. Draw a multi-colored pattern of shapes on white paper, using felt-tip pens. Study your design carefully through the different colored filters. Do the colors disappear? Do the colors change? Keep a record of which colors are affected by each filter.

2. "The train." Use the information you have discovered to make a disappearing picture.

3. Notice here how the green color shows up darkly through the red filter and the yellow and orange colors disappear.

4. Here, with the blue filter, the train has changed completely.

WARNING: NEVER HOLD PLASTIC OR CELLOPHANE RIGHT UP TO YOUR FACE.

Color weaving

You will need: two cardboard strips (approximately 7¾ × 1½ in), colored cellophane, double-sided adhesive tape.

1. Stick a strip of adhesive tape, 6¼ in long, along one edge of a cardboard strip. Cut four cellophane strips, 1½ in wide, in red, yellow, blue and green. Stick them side by side to the tape. Weave four cross-strips of cellophane in and out alternately, as shown.

2. Trim the first strips and attach these to the second cardboard strip at the base.

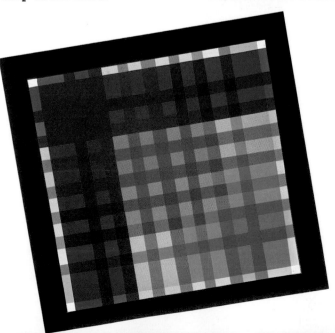

3. "Color square." Here the colored strips overlap each other in both directions. Notice how two layers of the same color deepen the color. How many different shades of color can you see?

PIGMENT

Pigmentation is the natural coloring of plants and minerals, and of the skins of people and animals.

Pigments (tiny particles of color) also give color to man-made paints and dyes. Paint colors are not so pure as light colors. You cannot mix paint color to obtain a yellow. Yellow, red and blue are the primary colors in paint.

Pigments reflect their own color and absorb the rest. When you mix paints or pigments, different colors are absorbed. If all the colors of the spectrum are mixed together all the colors will be absorbed and only black will remain.

Make a collection of objects and sort them by color. Look very closely at each object. Is the object naturally colored? Has the surface been painted, or is the color part of the material with which the object has been made?
Visit an art gallery and notice how different artists use color in their paintings. Look carefully at one painting. Is it brightly colored? Has the artist only used a limited range of colors?

Yellow, red and blue are the primary colors in paint.

Mixing paint colors

You will need: red, yellow and blue powder paint, a palette or plate, a paintbrush, water.

1. With a little water, mix some red and yellow paint together in equal proportions. Repeat with the blue and yellow, then the red and blue. What color is made if you mix all three colors together?

2. A color chart. Make your own chart to show the primary (red, yellow and blue) and secondary (orange, green and purple) paint colors. In the chart shown, the secondary colors have been mixed together also to produce the tertiary colors, browns and grays.

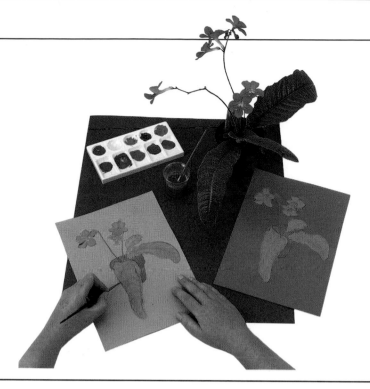

3. Experiment to see what color you obtain if you mix a primary color with a secondary color, such as red with orange. See how many different colors you can make by mixing just the three primary colors in different proportions. The variety is endless!

"Streptocarpus." Try to paint a picture of a plant using only the three primary colors. Can you mix the right amount of color to echo exactly the colors of the plant? Does the background color affect your painting?

How black is black?

You will need: different black colors such as pens, paints and inks, strips of blotting paper (or other absorbent paper), a bowl of water.

Is the black in pens and inks really black? You can use chromatography to test this.

Near one end of a strip of absorbent paper, draw and fill in a circle of black. Try to make the spots the same size for each black being tested. Suspend the strips over a bowl of water so that the edges of the paper just touch the water.

2. The water will be absorbed and move up the paper. The colors in the spots will be carried along the paper by the water and will separate. You will be able to see which colors were mixed together to make black.

1. Choose a selection of your own different black colors. Here a felt-tip pen, a ballpoint pen, paint and ink are being tested.

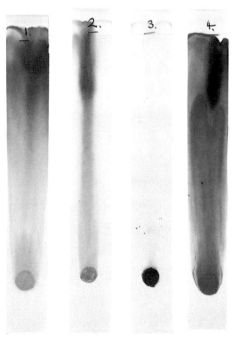

COLOR MEDIUMS

Artists use color in a variety of different mediums. Some color mediums are wet, such as paints, inks and dyes. Other color mediums are dry art materials. These include pencils, crayons, chalks and pastels.

Paint pigments are used in different mediums which bind the pigments together. This affects the style of painting, and how the artist works.

Watercolors are bound with a water-soluble medium such as gum arabic, and they dry quickly.

Acrylic paints are made by mixing the pigment with a PVA (polyvinyl acetate) medium. These can be worked thickly, and dry very quickly with a shiny finish.

Oil paints are pigments mixed with oil. They are bought as thick paint in tubes and can be thinned with linseed oil or white spirit. They dry very slowly.

Look at a colored wooden toy. Why would it not be sensible to color a wooden model with colored crayons?
Study a picture of an illuminated manuscript. Monks in the early Middle Ages decorated their books with fine watercolor paintings, often the first capital letter on a page and the margins of the pages. You could try to decorate your initials in a similar way.

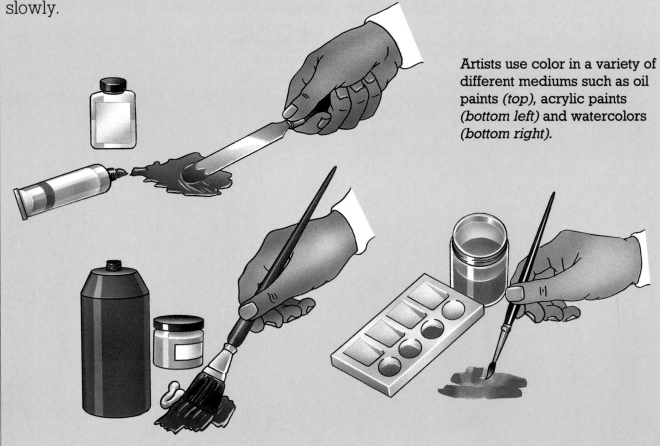

Artists use color in a variety of different mediums such as oil paints *(top)*, acrylic paints *(bottom left)* and watercolors *(bottom right)*.

Artists' colors – a test chart

You will need: a small quantity of colors in different wet and dry mediums.

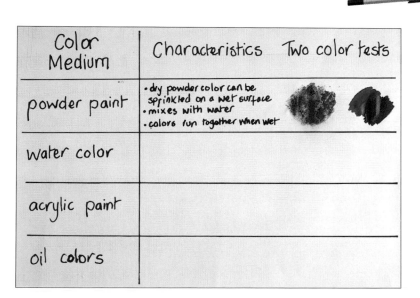

1. Test each color medium separately and make a chart of your results.

Color Medium	Characteristics	Two color tests
powder paint	• dry powder color can be sprinkled on a wet surface • mixes with water • colors run together when wet	
water color		
acrylic paint		
oil colors		

2. Think of some questions to ask about each medium. Here are some ideas. Wet colors: Do the colors run together? Do they dry quickly? What can you use to apply the color? How do you thin the color? Dry colors: Are they soft? Do they smudge? Do they blend together easily?

Color Medium	Characteristics	Two color tests
pencils	• a hard medium which can be sharpened to a point • clean to hold – wooden casing • colors do not run together	
chalk		
oil pastels		
wax crayons		

"Fun with color." Using powder color and colored papers

"St Paul's," using acrylic paints. These can be applied thickly and interesting textures can be created.

COLOR IN NATURE

Look at a garden, a field, the sky, the sea. You will see many colors. The colors you see will change as the light changes. In bright sunlight the colors are more brilliant. On a dark day, everything seems more gray.

Throughout the year, too, the colors in nature change as the plants, flowers and trees change with the seasons. Every plant, flower and animal has its own coloring. Studying their colors will help you to recognize them.

Spring

Summer

Fall

Find a stone. How many different colors can you see in it? Do the colors change if you make it wet?
Some flowers are red, for example, roses. Can you think of a flower for each color of the spectrum?

Throughout the year the color of many plants and trees changes with the seasons.

Camouflage

Some animals have colors that make them difficult to be seen in their natural surroundings. This is called camouflage. It helps them hide and keep safe from their enemies.

Sometimes camouflage helps animals to stalk their prey and get close without being seen. A polar bear is difficult to see against the arctic ice.

Leaf collage

You will need: a collection of leaves, white glue diluted with water to make a glaze, a paintbrush, paper.

1. Brush glaze over the surface of the paper and arrange your design of leaves. (This will be very sticky.) Coat each leaf with glaze and leave to dry.

2. The glaze will become shiny, and the leaves will be preserved as the air has been excluded. What do you think will happen to the leaves you have picked, but do not use?

3. Compare the two pictures. What do you notice about the colors of the leaves?

Camouflage experiment

You will need: an animal picture
(from an old magazine),
different colored paper.

Cut out your chosen animal
picture. Place it on different
colored background papers to
see which gives the most
camouflage. You could try to
create better camouflage by
adding some crayon details.

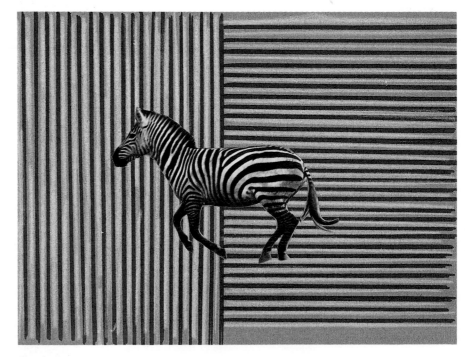

1. Lion. Which background
offers the lion better
camouflage?

2. Zebra. Why is it difficult to
see a zebra against a
background of black and white?
Would it be possible to
camouflage this zebra even
more with the black and white
crayons?

COLOR FROM NATURE

Long ago early painters obtained their colors from the materials around them. Reds and yellows came from the rocks and earth, blacks and grays from the ash and wood of their fires. Early hunters painted pictures of wild animals on the walls of their caves. The paintings were made using a mixture of colored earths and animal fats.

Dyes, too, can be obtained from nature. Before synthetic (man-made) dyes were invented, people used plant juices to dye their clothes. Some vegetable dyes are colorfast – the colors will not wash out – but most wash out easily unless a special fixer, called a mordant, is added.

Why do you think instructions for washing clothes advise you to separate light and dark colors? Have you ever spilled ink on the floor or a drink on your clothes? How difficult was it to wipe away the marks?

Dyes can be made by boiling plant material such as tea, beets, walnuts and onions.

Tea

Beets

Walnuts

Onions

Pictures from wood

You will need: a piece of burnt wood (such as from a campfire), some paper, a piece of broken branch, ash from a wood fire, cooking fat, a palette knife.

1. Find a piece of broken branch. Use your homemade charcoal (burnt wood) to make a sketch of the branch. Look carefully at the wood and notice how many colors there are.

2. You can experiment with cold wood ash too. A mixture of ash with a little cooking fat gives an interesting texture for artwork, and can be applied with a palette knife.

Make your own natural dyes

You will need: plant materials, (roots, leaves, fruit or bark), an old saucepan, water.

Put your chosen plant material into your saucepan with some water. Ask a grown-up to help you boil the plant material until the color moves from the plant to the water.

Leave the mixture to cool, then drain off the colored solution. Very often the colors obtained are shades of yellow and brown.

1. Boiling onion skins. These give a strong yellow dye which will give a permanent stain.

WARNING: REMEMBER THAT SOME PLANTS ARE PROTECTED SPECIES AND MUST NOT BE TAKEN FROM THE WILD.

ALSO, SOME PLANTS ARE POISONOUS SO CHECK WITH AN ADULT BEFORE PICKING ANYTHING.

2. Different dyes obtained from nature. From left to right: onion skins, laurel bark, dandelion roots, beets, tea, walnut shells, heather, lilac leaves.

Tie-dye

You will need: a bowl, your colored natural dyes, small pebbles or marbles, rubber bands, string, some pieces of cotton fabric, rubber gloves, an apron.

1. Tie your fabric in different ways. You can make knots, or tie it tightly with string as shown.

26

2. Here marbles are being placed in the fabric and held in position with rubber bands. Twist several rubber bands around each marble as tightly as you can.

3. Put on your apron and your rubber gloves to protect you and your clothes. Choose a colored dye and pour it into a bowl. Dip the fabric into the dye and push it down under the surface.

4. Allow the dye to soak into the fabric for a short while (about two minutes), then lift it out and leave it to dry. (The knotted square on the left has been soaked in onion dye).

6. "Flower design." White crayon drawing, painted with natural dyes

5. When the fabric is completely dry, remove the rubber bands and open it out. Notice how the rubber bands protected the fabric from the dye, giving an interesting pattern. Ask a grown-up to help you iron your fabric.

If you bend the spectrum of colors around into a circle, you will have a color wheel. The color wheel can help you choose colors that go well together. We call these colors harmonious. They are found next to each other on the color wheel.

Colors which lie opposite one another on the color wheel are called complementary colors. These dazzle the eye when they are put side by side.

Colors can affect our feelings. Harmonious colors put together are calming, but complementary colors startle and excite the senses.

A room decorated in pinks and reds feels warm, whereas a blue-colored room feels cold. Why do you think the quiet reading room in a library is not painted in bright complementary colors?

Look at a large street advertisement. Have bright, contrasting colors been used to attract the eye?

A dazzling pattern in contrasting colors.

A color wheel

1. Make your own color wheel. Oil pastels have been used for this wheel.

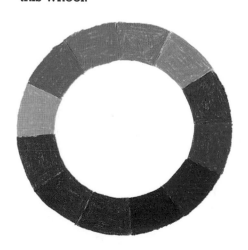

2. Experiment with pairs of harmonious colors and complementary colors. Which pairs of colors do you like together?

3. Which colors would you choose to decorate your bedroom and why?

4. Warm colors – and cool colors.

Make a picture using a limited palette.
An icy sea ...
... or tropical sun.

Black and white contrast

You will need: black paper (12 × 8¼ in.), white paper (16½ × 12 in.), a pencil, a ruler, scissors, cold water paste.

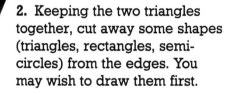

1. Fold a sheet of black paper in half. Draw a line from one corner to within ½ inch of the top of the fold. Cut out the triangle and cut along the fold. You now have two identical triangles.

2. Keeping the two triangles together, cut away some shapes (triangles, rectangles, semi-circles) from the edges. You may wish to draw them first.

3. Arrange and glue the cutout shapes on the piece of white paper so that they lie opposite to, and reflect, the spaces from which they were cut.

4. The finished design, showing the sharp contrast between black and white.

FURTHER IDEAS

Rainbow crayons

1. Testing the crayons

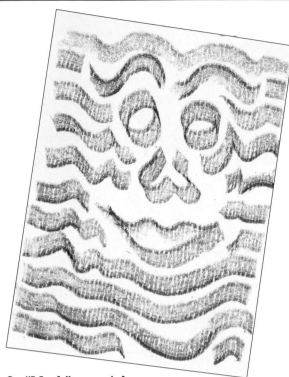

2. "Mask" – a rainbow crayon design

Fabric collage

You will need: different scraps of store-bought printed fabric, paper, scissors, white glue.

The colors used in the printed fabrics you have collected are permanent. They do not wash out like your natural dyes. Use your scraps to make a fabric collage.

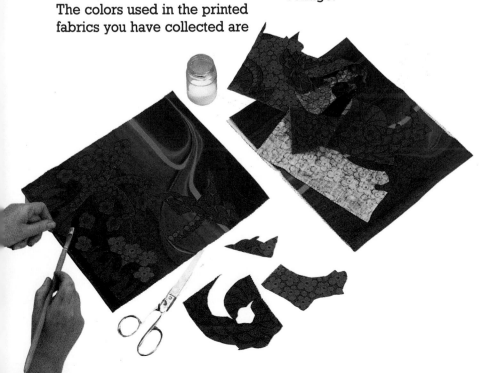

A photographic study

Use a camera to take photographs of color in our world. You can begin by using some of the ideas mentioned in each section of this book. Would it be possible to do this with a black and white film?

An illustrated dictionary

Make an illustrated dictionary of words that have links with color. Here are some examples:

colors in feelings: "green with envy," "seeing red "

colors in birds: blackbird, blue jay

colors in geography: the Black Forest, the Red Sea

GLOSSARY

Camouflage
The use of color by animals and plants to blend into their natural surroundings, so that they are "hidden."

Chromatography
A way of separating different colors.

Color
The sensation we perceive when light of different wavelengths falls on our eyes.

Color blindness
The inability to distinguish between certain colors. People who are color blind often cannot tell the difference between red and green.

Color schemes
Ordered arrangements of colors; for example, in decorating and furnishing a room.

Color vision
The ability of the human eye to detect differences in the wavelengths of light.

Color wheel
The colors of the spectrum joined around in a circle or wheel.

Complementary colors
These are opposite each other on the color wheel.

Dye
A color or stain used to change the color of a material. Dyes can be either natural or synthetic (man-made).

Filter
A colored screen (sometimes made of glass or cellophane) which allows only certain colors to pass through while absorbing others. It "filters" the light.

Harmonious colors
These are next to each other on the color wheel.

Medium
A substance which binds the colored pigment in artists' materials, such as the wax in wax crayons.

Mordant
A chemical substance which fixes the dye in the dyeing process. A mordant makes the color "fast" (colorfast), so that it will not run or fade.

Pigment
Small particles which give the color to different materials and substances. The coloring matter in paints and dyes.

Primary colors
In light, these are red, green and blue; in paints they are red, yellow and blue.

Refraction
Changing the direction of a beam of light, causing it to break up. When white light is refracted it can produce a spectrum.

Retina
The inside surface of the back of the eye which is sensitive to light. Different cells in the retina are sensitive to red, green and blue light.

Secondary colors
These are produced by mixing two primary colors together. They are yellow, cyan and magenta in light and orange, green and purple in paints.

Spectrum
A colored band of seven colors: red, orange, yellow, green, blue, indigo, violet. It is caused by the refraction of light. You can see the spectrum in a rainbow.

Tertiary colors
These are produced by mixing two secondary colors together. They are all grayish colors.

Wavelengths
Distances between points on the wave band along which light waves can be measured. The visible spectrum is in the middle wavelengths.

INDEX